DO YOU W...
**HaPPier,
HealtHier,
AND a
Better PERSON
OVERaLL?**

**THERE'S a
FREE AND SiMPLE
WaY THaT iS totally
YOUR CHOICE**

Gratitude is not an action.
It's an emotion.

It's the feeling of being thankful
and appreciative of what we
already have.

Gratitude is not just being
thankful for the big things in our
lives. It's about being grateful
and noticing the things that we
often take for granted.

We can multiply our happiness
and well-being with gratitude.

What is in this book?

Gratitude Journal

Journaling daily is very effective; doing it before bed will boost efficiency and enhance your sleep quality.

The daily prompt is to help you reflect on your memories and bring awareness of your surrounding and yourself. If you feel too stuck with the prompt of the day, flip to other pages for more inspiration.

Fun Facts & Quotes

Learn more about gratitude and its benefits and get inspired by others who practice being thankful.

Do-By-Yourself Activities

Bring more gratitude to your life with these fun activities you can do on your own.

Do-Together Activities

Use these activities to foster a culture of appreciation in your family, groups, and teams.

COLOUR YOUR PATH TO MINDFULNESS

You will see a lot of black-and-white doodle art throughout the book.

Colour your path to mindfulness – take a moment to slow down, be present, and remember the things we often take for granted.

 **KUDOS tO YOU!**

You're taking a beautiful step to nourish your well-being.

THIS BOOK BELONGS TO:

Letter of Appreciation

Take a moment to reflect – who has been there for you? Think of someone who has positively impacted your life.

Write that person a letter describing what they have done for you and why you feel grateful to them.

Who is this for?

_____

_____

_____

_____

_____

_____

_____

_____

_____

_____

_____

attitude of gratitude

improves **well-being** by

10%

which is the same impact as **doubling your income**

Gratitude

JOURNAL

Date: **S M T W T F S**

— MOOD-O-METER —

LOST   **MEH**   **FINE**   **GOOD**   **PERFECT**

What you want to say thanks to.

I'M THANKFUL FOR
these 3 things

→ _____

_____

→ _____

_____

→ _____

_____

What you feel appreciative for,
dive deeper and express why.

I'M GRATEFUL FOR
(a friend)

....

....

BECAUSE
....

....

....

....

....

....

Gratitude
JOURNAL

Date:

— MOOD-O-METER —

LOST   **MEH**   **FINE**   **GOOD**   **PERFECT**

I'M THANKFUL FOR

these 3 things

→ _____

_____

→ _____

_____

→ _____

_____

I'M GRATEFUL FOR
(a family member)

....

....

BECAUSE

....

....

....

....

....

....

I am happy because I'm grateful. I choose to be grateful. That gratitude allows me to be happy.

— Will Arnett —

Will Arnett is an actor and comedian known for his roles in shows like Arrested Development and BoJack Horseman. With his sharp wit and clever humour, Will brings joy and laughter to audiences around the world.

Gratitude
JOURNAL

Date:

S M T W T F S

— MOOD-O-METER —

LOST   MEH   FINE   GOOD   PERFECT

I'M THANKFUL FOR
these 3 things

→ _____

_____

→ _____

_____

→ _____

_____

I'M GRATEFUL FOR
(something useful)

....

....

BECAUSE
....

....

....

....

....

....

Gratitude
JOURNAL

Date:

S M T W T F S

— MOOD-O-METER —

LOST   **MEH**   **FINE**   **GOOD**   **PERFECT**

I'M THANKFUL FOR

these 3 things

→ _____

_____

→ _____

_____

→ _____

_____

I'M GRATEFUL FOR
(a knowledge)

....

....

BECAUSE
....

....

....

....

....

....

Gratitude
JOURNAL

Date:

S M T W T F S

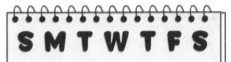

— MOOD-O-METER —

LOST **MEH** **FINE** **GOOD** **PERFECT**

I'M THANKFUL FOR
these *3* things

→ _____

_____

→ _____

_____

→ _____

_____

I'M GRATEFUL FOR
(something that always cheers me up)

....

....

BECAUSE
....

....

....

....

....

....

studies show that **3**
writing down things you're
GRATEFUL
✳ for every day for 21 days ✳
significantly increases your
OPTIMISM
⌇⌇⌇ at least for the next ⌇⌇⌇
6 MONtHS

FUN FACTS ★

Gratitude
JOURNAL

Date:

S M T W T F S

── MOOD-O-METER ──

LOST   **MEH**   **FINE**   **GOOD**   **PERFECT**

I'M THANKFUL FOR
these 3 things

→ _____

_____

→ _____

_____

→ _____

_____

I'M GRATEFUL FOR (something in the room/ place I am now)

....

....

BECAUSE ....

....

....

....

....

....

Gratitude

JOURNAL

Date:

S M T W T F S

── MOOD-O-METER ──

LOST **MEH** **FINE** **GOOD** **PERFECT**

I'M THANKFUL FOR
these 3 things

→ _____

_____

→ _____

_____

→ _____

_____

I'M GRATEFUL FOR
(a smell)

....

....

BECAUSE
....

....

....

....

....

There are so many things in the world that could be invisible to the material eye, and when you take a moment to stop, to pause, to be present and notice them —

that's gratitude.

— Jay Shetty —

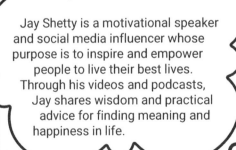

Jay Shetty is a motivational speaker and social media influencer whose purpose is to inspire and empower people to live their best lives. Through his videos and podcasts, Jay shares wisdom and practical advice for finding meaning and happiness in life.

Gratitude

JOURNAL

Date:

S M T W T F S

— MOOD-O-METER —

LOST   **MEH**   **FINE**   **GOOD**   **PERFECT**

I'M THANKFUL FOR

these 3 things

→ _____

_____

→ _____

_____

→ _____

_____

I'M GRATEFUL FOR
(something about the current season)

....

....

BECAUSE
....

....

....

....

....

....

....

Gratitude
JOURNAL

Date:

S M T W T F S

— MOOD-O-METER —

LOST   **MEH**   **FINE**   **GOOD**   **PERFECT**

I'M THANKFUL FOR

these 3 things

→ _____

_____

→ _____

_____

→ _____

_____

I'M GRATEFUL FOR
(something in nature)

....

....

BECAUSE ....

....

....

....

....

Flush Toilet

Have you flushed a toilet today? The fact that there is plumbing and water to give us that convenience is something to be thankful for. Flushing the toilet with a bucket of water every time after a "business" is no fun.

Sand

Sand is the world's most consumed raw material after water. Roads, bridges, silicon, glass, brick, mortar, and sandcastles are all created with sand. So next time you go to a beach, be grateful for this essential ingredient in our everyday lives.

Fingernails

Whether scratching an itch or scraping off those ridiculously sticky price tags – fingernails are just darn useful.

Gratitude
JOURNAL

Date:

S M T W T F S

— MOOD-O-METER —

LOST   **MEH**   **FINE**   **GOOD**   **PERFECT**

I'M THANKFUL FOR
these 3 things

→ _____

_____

→ _____

_____

→ _____

_____

I'M GRATEFUL FOR
(a talent I have)

....

....

BECAUSE
....

....

....

....

....

....

Gratitude

JOURNAL

Date:

S M T W T F S

—— MOOD-O-METER ——

LOST   **MEH**   **FINE**   **GOOD**   **PERFECT**

I'M THANKFUL FOR
these 3 things

→ _____

_____

→ _____

_____

→ _____

_____

I'M GRATEFUL FOR
(something makes me laugh)

....

....

BECAUSE
....

....

....

....

....

....

Gratitude
JOURNAL

Date:

S M T W T F S

— MOOD-O-METER —

LOST　**MEH**　**FINE**　**GOOD**　**PERFECT**

I'M THANKFUL FOR
these 3 things

→ _____

_____

→ _____

_____

→ _____

_____

I'M GRATEFUL FOR
(a person who bring you joy)

....

....

BECAUSE
....

....

....

....

....

HAPPY

people's **income** is

roughly **7%** ↑HIGHER

FUN FACTS ★

Gratitude
JOURNAL

Date:

S M T W T F S

— MOOD-O-METER —

LOST   MEH   FINE   GOOD   PERFECT

I'M THANKFUL FOR

these 3 things

→ _____

_____

→ _____

_____

→ _____

_____

I'M GRATEFUL FOR
(a game/ toy)

....

....

BECAUSE

....

....

....

....

....

....

Gratitude

JOURNAL

Date:

S M T W T F S

— MOOD-O-METER —

LOST　　**MEH**　　**FINE**　　**GOOD**　　**PERFECT**

I'M THANKFUL FOR

these 3 things

→ _____

_____

→ _____

_____

→ _____

_____

I'M GRATEFUL FOR
(a colour)

....

....

BECAUSE
....

....

....

....

....

....

Gratitude ABC's

Go through the alphabet and describe what you are thankful for. For example, "D for dogs giving unconditional love."

A _____
B _____
C _____
D _____
E _____
F _____
G _____
H _____
I _____
J _____
K _____
L _____
M _____

N _____
O _____
P _____
Q _____
R _____
S _____
T _____
U _____
V _____
W _____
X _____
Y _____
Z _____

Gratitude
JOURNAL

Date:

S M T W T F S

—— MOOD-O-METER ——

LOST   **MEH**   **FINE**   **GOOD**   **PERFECT**

I'M THANKFUL FOR
these 3 things

→ _____

_____

→ _____

_____

→ _____

_____

I'M GRATEFUL FOR
(something inspires me)

....

....

BECAUSE
....

....

....

....

....

....

Gratitude
JOURNAL

Date:

S M T W T F S

— MOOD-O-METER —

LOST　　**MEH**　　**FINE**　　**GOOD**　**PERFECT**

I'M THANKFUL FOR

these 3 things

→ _____

_____

→ _____

_____

→ _____

_____

I'M GRATEFUL FOR
(a sound)

....

....

BECAUSE
....

....

....

....

....

....

Always have an attitude of gratitude.

— Sterling K. Brown —

Sterling K. Brown is an actor known for his powerful performances in shows like This Is Us and The People v. O.J. Simpson: American Crime Story. With his talent and dedication, Sterling brings depth and humanity to every role he plays.

Gratitude
JOURNAL

Date:

S M T W T F S

— MOOD-O-METER —

LOST   MEH   FINE   GOOD   PERFECT

I'M THANKFUL FOR
these 3 things

→ _____

_____

→ _____

_____

→ _____

_____

I'M GRATEFUL FOR
(a tradition)

....

....

BECAUSE
....

....

....

....

....

....

Gratitude
JOURNAL

Date:

S M T W T F S

— MOOD-O-METER —

LOST   MEH   FINE   GOOD   PERFECT

I'M THANKFUL FOR
these 3 things

→ _____

_____

→ _____

_____

→ _____

_____

I'M GRATEFUL FOR
(a book/ article)

....

....

BECAUSE   ....

....

....

....

....

....

Gratitude
JOURNAL

Date:

S M T W T F S

— MOOD-O-METER —

LOST **MEH** **FINE** **GOOD** **PERFECT**

I'M THANKFUL FOR

these 3 things

→ _____

_____

→ _____

_____

→ _____

_____

I'M GRATEFUL FOR
(a hobby)

....

....

BECAUSE
....

....

....

....

....

....

studies show that it is
IMPOSSIBLE
to **feel depressed** and
GRATEFUL
at the same moment

While practicing **gratitude can't**
FIX DEPRESSION
it is **helpful** as a part of a
comprehensive treatment plan

FUN FACTS ★

Gratitude

JOURNAL

Date:

S M T W T F S

— MOOD-O-METER —

LOST   **MEH**   **FINE**   **GOOD**   **PERFECT**

I'M THANKFUL FOR
these 3 things

→ _____
_____

→ _____
_____

→ _____
_____

I'M GRATEFUL FOR
(something fun)

....

....

BECAUSE
....

....

....

....

....

Gratitude

JOURNAL

Date:

S M T W T F S
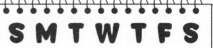

—— MOOD-O-METER ——

LOST   **MEH**   **FINE**   **GOOD**   **PERFECT**

I'M THANKFUL FOR

these 3 things

→ _____

_____

→ _____

_____

→ _____

_____

I'M GRATEFUL FOR
(a neighbour or a friend)

....

....

BECAUSE
....

....

....

....

....

....

MINDFULNESS DOODLING

Doodle something...

○ that makes you happy.

○ you can't live without.

○ that makes you smile.

○ you love to do.

○ you think is fun.

○ that makes you feel good.

○ that makes you laugh.

○ you are thankful for.

Gratitude
JOURNAL

Date:

S M T W T F S

— MOOD-O-METER —

LOST   MEH   FINE   GOOD   PERFECT

I'M THANKFUL FOR
these 3 things

→ _____

_____

→ _____

_____

→ _____

_____

I'M GRATEFUL FOR
(something about my school/ work)

....

....

BECAUSE
....

....

....

....

....

....

....

Gratitude
JOURNAL

Date: | **S M T W T F S**

— MOOD-O-METER —

LOST   **MEH**   **FINE**   **GOOD**   **PERFECT**

I'M THANKFUL FOR
these 3 things

→ _____

_____

→ _____

_____

→ _____

_____

I'M GRATEFUL FOR
(a skill I have)

....

....

BECAUSE
....

....

....

....

....

....

When life is sweet, say thank you and celebrate. When life is bitter, say thank you and grow.

— Shauna Niequist —

Shauna Niequist is a bestselling author and speaker known for her honest and vulnerable writing about faith, food, and family. Her words have inspired countless readers to live more fully and cultivate gratitude in their own lives.

Gratitude

JOURNAL

Date: | **S M T W T F S**
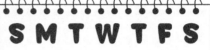

— MOOD-O-METER —

LOST **MEH** **FINE** **GOOD** **PERFECT**

I'M THANKFUL FOR
these 3 things

→ _____

_____

→ _____

_____

→ _____

_____

I'M GRATEFUL FOR
(something I have learned)

....

....

BECAUSE
....

....

....

....

....

Gratitude

JOURNAL

Date:

S M T W T F S

— MOOD-O-METER —

LOST   MEH   FINE   GOOD   PERFECT

I'M THANKFUL FOR

these 3 things

→ _____

_____

→ _____

_____

→ _____

_____

I'M GRATEFUL FOR
(a city or a town)

....

....

BECAUSE
....

....

....

....

....

....

Gratitude
JOURNAL

Date:

S M T W T F S

— MOOD-O-METER —

LOST   **MEH**   **FINE**   **GOOD**   **PERFECT**

I'M THANKFUL FOR
these 3 things

→ _____

_____

→ _____

_____

→ _____

_____

I'M GRATEFUL FOR
(a type of weather)

....

....

BECAUSE
....

....

....

....

....

....

GRATITUDE REWIRES YOUR BRAIN TO HAPPINESS

A LOOK AT HOW GRATITUDE WORKS INSIDE OUR BRAINS

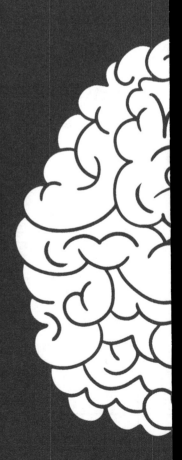

FUN FACTS ⭐

In observations of our brain in action, the brain regions hippocampus and amygdala light up during grateful moments. It triggers the brain's reward path, puts the emotion-regulating sites at work and kickstarts the production of dopamine, serotonin and oxytocin. These neuro-transmitters are what make us feel good.

These "feel good" chemicals activate the left prefrontal cortex of the brain, creating feelings of happiness and contentment. However, it is impossible to continuously exist in a happy state full-time because our brain has finite supplies of the "feel good" chemicals.

Nevertheless, everything you need to be happy is already inside your brain. Trigger those "feel good" neurotransmitters by practicing gratitude – you can improve sleep, boost happiness and enhance your well-being overall.

Gratitude
JOURNAL

Date: |

S M T W T F S

— MOOD-O-METER —

LOST   **MEH**   **FINE**   **GOOD**   **PERFECT**

I'M THANKFUL FOR

these 3 things

→ _____

_____

→ _____

_____

→ _____

_____

I'M GRATEFUL FOR
(a small thing)

....

....

BECAUSE
....

....

....

....

....

....

Gratitude
JOURNAL

Date:

S M T W T F S

— MOOD-O-METER —

LOST   **MEH**   **FINE**   **GOOD**   **PERFECT**

I'M THANKFUL FOR

these 3 things

→ _____

_____

→ _____

_____

→ _____

_____

I'M GRATEFUL FOR
(something I can do)

....

....

BECAUSE
....

....

....

....

....

....

Mindfulness Thank You Community Helper Poster

Recognize a key worker in your community by creating a thank-you keepsake.

Think about who keeps your community operational, safe and healthy. Doodle around the thank-you text, add some colours, cut out the poster and give it to the community helper you like to thank.

Gratitude

JOURNAL

Date: | **S M T W T F S**

— MOOD-O-METER —

LOST   **MEH**   **FINE**   **GOOD**   **PERFECT**

I'M THANKFUL FOR
these 3 things

→ _____

_____

→ _____

_____

→ _____

_____

I'M GRATEFUL FOR
(something is done for me)

....

....

BECAUSE
....

....

....

....

....

....

Gratitude
JOURNAL

Date: | S M T W T F S

— MOOD-O-METER —

LOST **MEH** **FINE** **GOOD** **PERFECT**

I'M THANKFUL FOR
these 3 things

→ _____

_____

→ _____

_____

→ _____

_____

I'M GRATEFUL FOR
(someone taught me something)

....

....

BECAUSE
....

....

....

....

....

....

Gratitude and attitude are not challenges; they are choices.

— Robert Braathe —

Robert Braathe is a business coach and author who helps entrepreneurs and professionals grow their businesses and achieve their goals. With his practical and inspiring advice, Robert empowers people to reach their full potential and succeed in their careers.

Gratitude
JOURNAL

Date:

S M T W T F S

— MOOD-O-METER —

LOST   MEH   FINE   GOOD   PERFECT

I'M THANKFUL FOR

these 3 things

→ _____

_____

→ _____

_____

→ _____

_____

I'M GRATEFUL FOR
(an animal)

....

....

BECAUSE
....

....

....

....

....

....

Gratitude

JOURNAL

Date:

S M T W T F S

—— MOOD-O-METER ——

LOST **MEH** **FINE** **GOOD** **PERFECT**

I'M THANKFUL FOR
these 3 things

→ _____

_____

→ _____

_____

→ _____

_____

I'M GRATEFUL FOR
(a way I can help others)

....

....

BECAUSE
....

....

....

....

....

....

Gratitude
JOURNAL

Date: _____

S M T W T F S

— MOOD-O-METER —

LOST　　**MEH**　　**FINE**　　**GOOD**　**PERFECT**

I'M THANKFUL FOR

these 3 things

→ _____

_____

→ _____

_____

→ _____

_____

I'M GRATEFUL FOR
(something that makes me feel safe)

....

....

BECAUSE
....

....

....

....

....

....

studies show that

gratitude and appreciation

can boost your |||||||||||||||||||||||||||||||||||

SELF-ESTEEM

FUN FACTS ⭐

Gratitude

JOURNAL

Date:

S M T W T F S

── MOOD-O-METER ──

LOST   **MEH**   **FINE**   **GOOD**   **PERFECT**

I'M THANKFUL FOR

these 3 things

→ _____

_____

→ _____

_____

→ _____

_____

I'M GRATEFUL FOR
(something outside)

....

....

BECAUSE
....

....

....

....

....

....

GratitUDE

JOURNAL

Date:

S M T W T F S

─── MOOD-O-METER ───

LOST   **MEH**   **FINE**   **GOOD**   **PERFECT**

I'M THANKFUL FOR
these 3 things

→ _____

_____

→ _____

_____

→ _____

_____

I'M GRATEFUL FOR
(something beautiful)

....

....

BECAUSE
....

....

....

....

....

....

Gratitude Maze Treasure Hunt

Gratitude is also about being thankful for the little things.

Find your paths on the maze, take time to complete each task and take a picture of what you find.

Once you finish the treasure hunt, you can turn the images into a digital or printed photo collage as your gratitude reminder or, share it with your friends and family.

Gratitude
JOURNAL

Date:

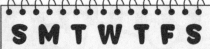

S M T W T F S

— MOOD-O-METER —

LOST　　**MEH**　　**FINE**　　**GOOD**　　**PERFECT**

I'M THANKFUL FOR

these 3 things

→ _____

_____

→ _____

_____

→ _____

_____

I'M GRATEFUL FOR
(a holiday)

....

....

BECAUSE
....

....

....

....

....

....

Gratitude

JOURNAL

Date: _____

S M T W T F S

— MOOD-O-METER —

LOST   **MEH**   **FINE**   **GOOD**   **PERFECT**

I'M THANKFUL FOR

these 3 things

→ _____

_____

→ _____

_____

→ _____

_____

I'M GRATEFUL FOR
(a food)

....

....

BECAUSE
....

....

....

....

....

Enjoy the little things, for one day you may look back and realize they were the big things.

— Robert Brault —

Robert Brault is a writer and philosopher whose words have inspired readers around the world to see beauty in the ordinary and find joy in the present moment. With his wisdom and wit, Robert encourages us to live fully and appreciate the beauty of everyday life.

Gratitude

JOURNAL

Date:

S M T W T F S

— MOOD-O-METER —

LOST   **MEH**   **FINE**   **GOOD**   **PERFECT**

I'M THANKFUL FOR
these 3 things

→ _____

_____

→ _____

_____

→ _____

_____

I'M GRATEFUL FOR
(a memory)

....

....

BECAUSE
....

....

....

....

....

....

Gratitude
JOURNAL

Date:

S M T W T F S

— MOOD-O-METER —

LOST   **MEH**   **FINE**   **GOOD**   **PERFECT**

I'M THANKFUL FOR
these 3 things

→ _____

_____

→ _____

_____

→ _____

_____

I'M GRATEFUL FOR
(a teacher/ mentor/ coach)

....

....

BECAUSE
....

....

....

....

....

....

Gratitude

JOURNAL

Date:

S M T W T F S

— MOOD-O-METER —

LOST　　**MEH**　　**FINE**　　**GOOD**　**PERFECT**

I'M THANKFUL FOR
these 3 things

→ _____

_____

→ _____

_____

→ _____

_____

I'M GRATEFUL FOR
(a tool)

....

....

BECAUSE
....

....

....

....

....

....

Gratitude improves

RELATIONSHIPS

Youths who live gratefully have

13% fewer fights

FUN FACTS ⭐

Gratitude
JOURNAL

Date:

S M T W T F S

— MOOD-O-METER —

LOST   MEH   FINE   GOOD   PERFECT

I'M THANKFUL FOR
these 3 things

→ _____

_____

→ _____

_____

→ _____

_____

I'M GRATEFUL FOR
(something that makes my life easier)

....

....

BECAUSE ....

....

....

....

....

....

Gratitude
JOURNAL

Date:

S M T W T F S

— MOOD-O-METER —

LOST **MEH** **FINE** **GOOD** **PERFECT**

I'M THANKFUL FOR

these 3 things

→ _____

_____

→ _____

_____

→ _____

_____

I'M GRATEFUL FOR (something makes me happy to be alive)

....

....

BECAUSE ....

....

....

....

....

....

Gratitude Slips

Pass a slip along and share your gratitude with others.

Let's Practice

THANK YOU FOR LISTENING TO ME.

THANK YOU FOR HELPING ME.

I'M THANKFUL FOR YOUR SENSE OF HUMOUR.

I'M GRATEFUL FOR WHO YOU ARE.

I APPRECIATE WHAT YOU DID FOR ME.

THANKS FOR BEING KIND TO ME.

THANK YOU FOR MAKING ME LAUGH.

THANK YOU FOR BEING A GOOD FRIEND.

THANK YOU FOR BEING YOU.

THANK YOU FOR ALL YOU HAVE DONE FOR ME.

THANKS FOR MAKING ME SMILE.

THANKS FOR EVERYTHING.

THANK YOU FOR BEING THERE FOR ME.

THANK YOU FOR

THANK YOU FOR

Gratitude
JOURNAL

Date:

S M T W T F S

—— MOOD-O-METER ——

LOST   MEH   FINE   GOOD   PERFECT

I'M THANKFUL FOR

these 3 things

→ _____

_____

→ _____

_____

→ _____

_____

I'M GRATEFUL FOR
(something inside)

....

....

BECAUSE
....

....

....

....

....

....

Gratitude
JOURNAL

Date:

S M T W T F S

—— MOOD-O-METER ——

LOST   **MEH**   **FINE**   **GOOD**   **PERFECT**

I'M THANKFUL FOR
these 3 things

→ _____

_____

→ _____

_____

→ _____

_____

I'M GRATEFUL FOR
(an event)

....

....

BECAUSE
....

....

....

....

....

....

I am grateful for all of my problems. After each one was overcome, I became stronger and more able to meet those that were still to come. I grew in all my difficulties.

— J.C. Penney —

J.C. Penney was a successful businessman and philanthropist who founded the department store chain that bears his name. His innovative business strategies and commitment to customer service have helped shape the modern retail industry and made him a respected and influential figure.

Gratitude
JOURNAL

Date:

—— MOOD-O-METER ——

LOST   MEH   FINE   GOOD   PERFECT

I'M THANKFUL FOR
these 3 things

→ _____

_____

→ _____

_____

→ _____

_____

I'M GRATEFUL FOR
(something in my home)

....

....

BECAUSE
....

....

....

....

....

....

Gratitude
JOURNAL

Date:

S M T W T F S

—— MOOD-O-METER ——

LOST   **MEH**   **FINE**   **GOOD**   **PERFECT**

I'M THANKFUL FOR

these 3 things

→ _____

_____

→ _____

_____

→ _____

_____

I'M GRATEFUL FOR
(something about me)

....

....

BECAUSE
....

....

....

....

....

....

Gratitude
JOURNAL

Date:

S M T W T F S

— MOOD-O-METER —

LOST   MEH   FINE   GOOD   PERFECT

I'M THANKFUL FOR
these 3 things

→ _____

_____

→ _____

_____

→ _____

_____

I'M GRATEFUL FOR
(a person I met recently)

....

....

BECAUSE
....

....

....

....

....

....

the **most grateful**
countries are
S. Africa, UAE, Philippines & India

Overall **positive emotions** can add up to **7 YEARS** to your life

FUN FACTS ★

Gratitude
JOURNAL

Date:

S M T W T F S

— MOOD-O-METER —

LOST   **MEH**   **FINE**   **GOOD**   **PERFECT**

I'M THANKFUL FOR

these 3 things

→ _____

_____

→ _____

_____

→ _____

_____

I'M GRATEFUL FOR
(a place)

....

....

BECAUSE
....

....

....

....

....

....

Gratitude
JOURNAL

Date:

S M T W T F S

—— MOOD-O-METER ——

LOST　　**MEH**　　**FINE**　　**GOOD**　　**PERFECT**

I'M THANKFUL FOR

these 3 things

→ _____

_____

→ _____

_____

→ _____

_____

I'M GRATEFUL FOR
(a song/ music)

....

....

BECAUSE
....

....

....

....

....

....

Prepare these mini place cards before you have dinner with others. Start by cutting out the cards and folding them in half. Write the names of the people you see on the front of the cards and add thankful messages inside.

Place the cards on the table before the meal. As a bonus, go around the table during the dinner and invite everyone to read out their messages. Then ask them to share one thing they are grateful for.

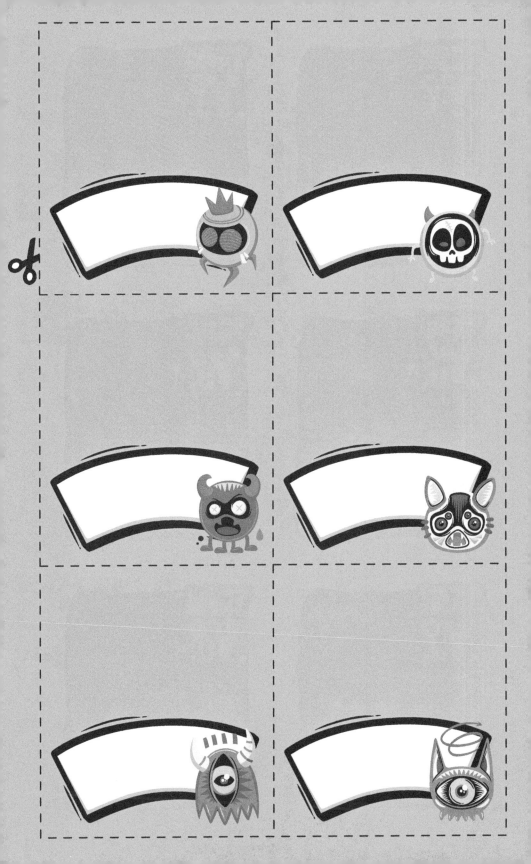

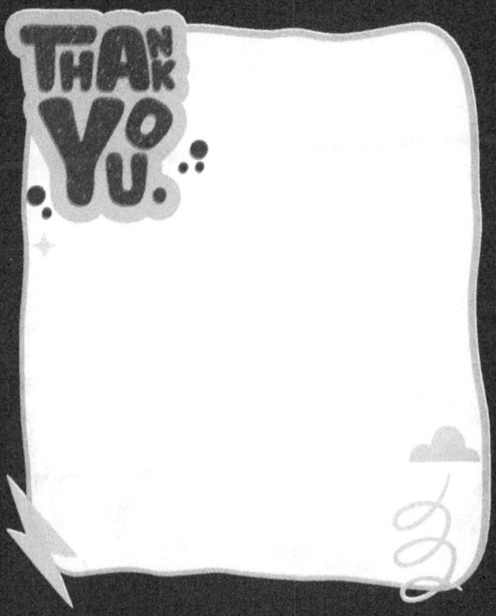
THANK YOU.
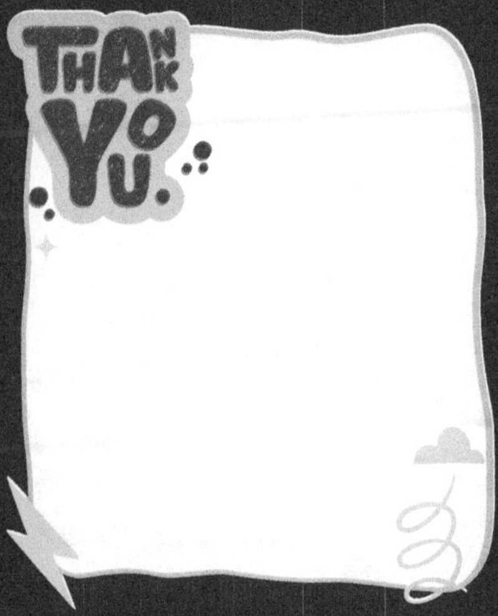
THANK YOU.
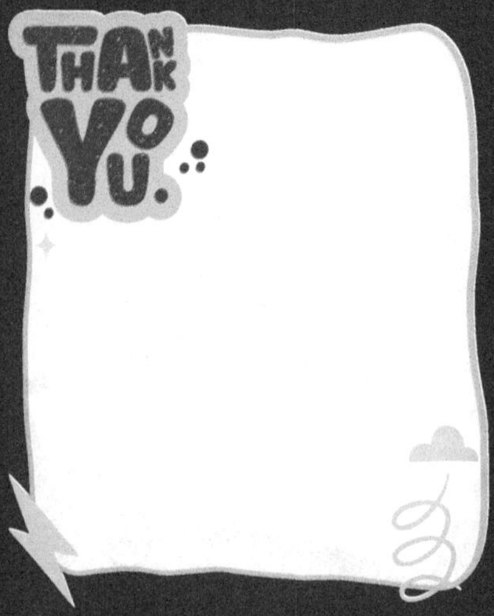
THANK YOU.
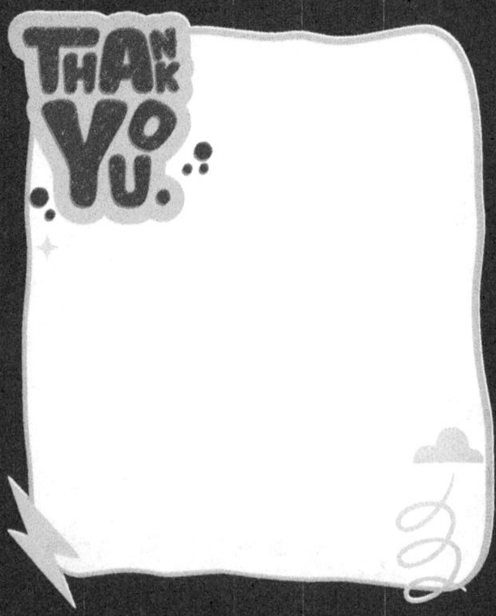
THANK YOU.
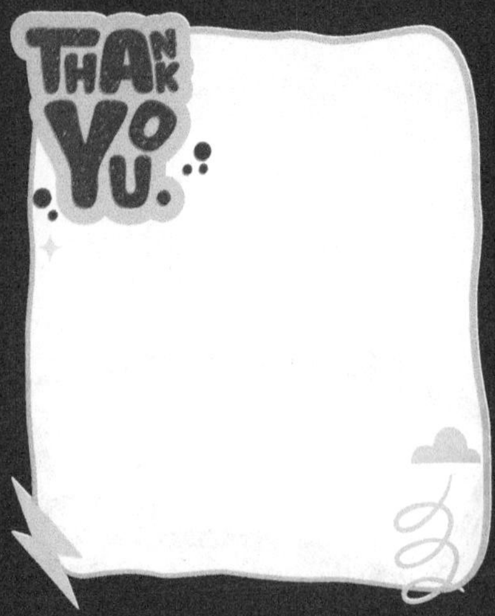
THANK YOU.
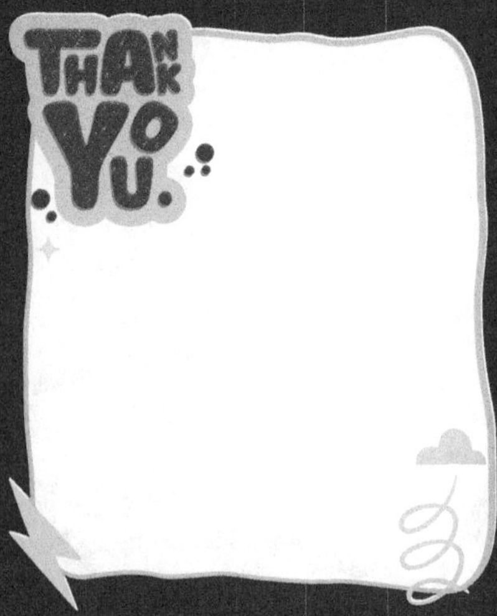
THANK YOU.

Gratitude
JOURNAL

Date:

S M T W T F S

— MOOD-O-METER —

LOST   **MEH**   **FINE**   **GOOD**   **PERFECT**

I'M THANKFUL FOR
these 3 things

→ _____

_____

→ _____

_____

→ _____

_____

I'M GRATEFUL FOR
(simple pleasure)

....

....

BECAUSE
....

....

....

....

....

....

Gratitude
JOURNAL

Date:

S M T W T F S

— MOOD-O-METER —

LOST   **MEH**   **FINE**   **GOOD**   **PERFECT**

I'M THANKFUL FOR

these 3 things

→ _____

_____

→ _____

_____

→ _____

_____

I'M GRATEFUL FOR (something about your body or your health)

....

....

BECAUSE

....

....

....

....

....

....

Be thankful for what you have; you'll end up having more. If you concentrate on what you don't have, you will never, ever have enough.

— Oprah Winfrey —

Oprah Winfrey is a media mogul, actress, and philanthropist whose purpose is to inspire and empower people to live their best lives. Through her television show, magazine, and various business ventures, Oprah has touched the hearts and minds of millions of people around the world.

Gratitude

JOURNAL

Date:

S M T W T F S

——— MOOD-O-METER ———

LOST   MEH   FINE   GOOD   PERFECT

I'M THANKFUL FOR
these 3 things

→ _____

_____

→ _____

_____

→ _____

_____

I'M GRATEFUL FOR
(something I can see)

....

....

BECAUSE
....

....

....

....

....

....

Gratitude
JOURNAL

Date:

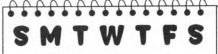
S M T W T F S

——— MOOD-O-METER ———

LOST　　**MEH**　　**FINE**　　**GOOD**　　**PERFECT**

I'M THANKFUL FOR

these 3 things

→ _____

_____

→ _____

_____

→ _____

_____

I'M GRATEFUL FOR
(an opportunity I have)

....

....

BECAUSE
....

....

....

....

....

....

Gratitude
JOURNAL

Date:

S M T W T F S

— MOOD-O-METER —

LOST   MEH   FINE   GOOD   PERFECT

I'M THANKFUL FOR
these 3 things

→ _____

_____

→ _____

_____

→ _____

_____

I'M GRATEFUL FOR
(something on my desk)

....

....

BECAUSE

....

....

....

....

....

research shows that

Gratitude increases by

5%

for every

10 YEARS

you get older

FUN FACTS ★

Gratitude

JOURNAL

Date:

S M T W T F S

— MOOD-O-METER —

LOST   **MEH**   **FINE**   **GOOD**   **PERFECT**

I'M THANKFUL FOR

these 3 things

→ _____

_____

→ _____

_____

→ _____

_____

I'M GRATEFUL FOR
(the best gift I have ever received)

....

....

BECAUSE

....

....

....

....

....

....

Gratitude
JOURNAL

Date:

S M T W T F S

—— MOOD-O-METER ——

LOST **MEH** **FINE** **GOOD** **PERFECT**

I'M THANKFUL FOR

these 3 things

→ _____

_____

→ _____

_____

→ _____

_____

I'M GRATEFUL FOR
(something that makes me smile)

....

....

BECAUSE

....

....

....

....

....

....

Gratitude Summary Poster

Recap all the things you have written in your gratitude journal, or take some time to reflect on other things you are thankful for. Write them on the dotted lines to create a poster.

I AM GRATEFUL FOR

BE ABLE TO FEEL PAIN
the anonymous acts of kindness

THE ABILITY TO WORK WITH MY HANDS
scissors to help me open all the packages

UNCONTROLLABLE LAUGHTER
ink so we print and paint

FUZZY SOCKS
the dishwashers save relationships

A GOOD NIGHT'S SLEEP
my soft pillow

DIVERSITY
digital memory

HAPPY HOURS
indoor toilets

MY FAMILY
social media

ALARM CLOCK
breath refresher

HOT SHOWERS
farmers markets

NETFLIX
my comfy shoes

CAMPFIRES
salt

MY EDUCATION
the world has colours

FREEDOM OF RELIGION
the undo function on the computer

FOOD DELIVERY SERVICES
my well-designed hair dryer

MY JOB AS A MONSTER MAKER
fortune cookies with perfectly timed fortunes

SUCCESSFULLY MAKING SAMOSA
seeing something from a new angle

THE PANCAKE FROM MASS
those long, late-night conversations

HAVE GOOPAW AS MY CLOSE FRIEND
checking something off my to-do list

INDOOR PLUMBING FOR FLUSHING TOILET
driving and getting nothing but green lights

PARIS HOLIDAY WITH FAMILY
finally getting to wear my favourite sweater

MY COMFY COUCH
a nice cup of hot chocolate

THE PAVEMENT
Smogfang is my neighbour

THE INTERNET
my umbrella

I CAN READ
digital photographs

MY HEALTH
family dinners

SPELL CHECK
chocolate cakes

TOILET PAPER
seeing my pet

DUCT TAPE
last road trip

CLEAN WATER
having choices

ABILITY TO GIVE GIFTS
heartfelt apologies

PUBLIC TRANSPORTATION
battery to power my electronics

LEARNING FROM UNIQUE CULTURES
Zipper saving us from buttoning up our jeans and jackets

CLOTHES FRESH OUT OF THE DRYER
the human capacity to be thankful

MODERN HEALTHCARE
hugs to keep us from feeling lonely

I CAN GOOGLE ANY QUESTION
body hair to keep us warm

A Thank-you Letter to Myself

Having gratitude for others is essential, but appreciating yourself is even more important, as no one else can do that for you.

Pick a place where you feel comfortable. Write a thank-you letter to yourself to pause, reflect, and appreciate who you are. The more specific, the more impactful it will be. This exercise may not be easy but it will be well worth the effort.

_____

_____

_____

_____

_____

_____

_____

_____

_____

_____

_____

_____

_____

DO-TOGETHER ACTIVITIES

 **Let's practice**

Gratitude Tic-Tac-Toe

Practice gratitude with this fun and easy Tic-Tac-Toe group activity.

Take turns responding to the prompt to claim the spot with an X or an O. The player who succeeds in placing three of their marks in a horizontal, vertical, or diagonal row wins.

SOMETHING IN NATURE	A PERSON	A MEMORY
SOMETHING MONEY CAN'T BUY	A CHALLENGE	A STRENGTH
A PLACE	A FUNNY THING	AN UNCON-VENTIONAL THING

A STRENGTH	A PLACE	AN UNCON-VENTIONAL THING
A CHALLENGE	A PERSON	SOMETHING IN NATURE
SOMETHING MONEY CAN'T BUY	A MEMORY	A FUNNY THING

AN UNCON-VENTIONAL THING	SOMETHING IN NATURE	A PERSON
A STRENGTH	A FUNNY THING	A PLACE
A CHALLENGE	SOMETHING MONEY CAN'T BUY	A MEMORY

A MEMORY	SOMETHING MONEY CAN'T BUY	A FUNNY THING
A PLACE	A STRENGTH	AN UNCON-VENTIONAL THING
A PERSON	SOMETHING IN NATURE	A CHALLENGE

Let's practice

Gather a group of 3 to 6 players and have fun while sharing gratitude together.

Set a timer for 20 minutes. Every player takes turns rolling the dice. The first roll is for the row number, and the second is for the column number. Alternatively, you could cut out the numbers on the page, fold them up, put them in a bag or an envelope and draw from it.

Use the drawn row number and column number, find the intersection on the grid, and follow the instruction on the field.

Track the points of each player. The game ends at the end of the 20 minutes and the player with the most points wins.

	1	2	3	4	5	6
1	+3 points Name a person you are thankful for (and why)	+2 points	+3 points Share an emotion you are thankful for	+2 points Name a holiday you are thankful for	+1 point	+3 points Share an activity you are thankful for (and why)
2	+4 points Share a memory you are thankful for (and why)	+2 points Share an experience you are thankful for	+2 points Name an atmosphere you are thankful for	+3 points	+2 points Name a drink you are thankful for	**Pause your next turn**
3	+1 point Name a book you are thankful for	+4 points and have another roll/draw	+3 points	+4 points Name a person who inspired you (and why)	+1 points	+2 points Name something fun you're thankful for
4	+3 points	+3 points Share a vacation memory you are thankful for	+4 points Thank yourself for something	+2 points	+3 points Name an ability you are thankful for	+1 points
5	+3 points Name a food you are thankful for	+2 points	+2 points Name a gift you are thankful for	+2 points and have another roll/draw	+4 points Share an invisible thing you are thankful for	+2 points Name something that makes you happy
6	+2 points and have another roll/draw	+2 points Name a sound you are thankful for	+3 points	+3 points Share a moment when someone helped you	+3 points and pause your next turn	+3 points Name anything you are thankful for (and why)

1 2 3 4 5 6

Gratitude Conversation Starter

Remember all the little things to be grateful for in your wonderful lives with these gratitude conversation starters.

Cut out the strips, fold them, and put them in a jar. Take turns to pull out a strip and have everyone answer during dinner or a long car trip. Let the conversation flow.

WHAT IS SOMETHING YOU LOVE DOING WITH YOUR FAMILY?

HOW DOES IT FEEL TO DO SOMETHING NICE FOR SOMEONE?

WHAT IS YOUR FAVOURITE PART ABOUT YOUR HOME? WHY?

WHAT ARE THREE THINGS YOU ARE GRATEFUL FOR TODAY?

WHAT WAS YOUR FAVOURITE PART ABOUT THIS WEEK?

WHAT IS YOUR FAVOURITE THING ABOUT TODAY AND WHY?

HOW DID YOU HELP SOMEONE RECENTLY?

WHAT ABILITIES DO HUMANS HAVE YOU ARE GRATEFUL FOR?

WHO DID SOMETHING NICE FOR YOU RECENTLY? WHAT WAS IT?

Colour Object Collecting Gratitude Game

Each player takes a turn to collect an object in your environment that is one of these colours: red, orange, purple, brown, blue, or green.

An important rule is to keep everything else in order, and you must name what you are grateful for based on its colour and categories. Otherwise, you lose your turn and won't get the object.

The player that collects the most objects wins the game in the end.

When you finish the game, you can take a picture with all the collected objects to remember the fun and gratitude you shared with your peers, friends or family.

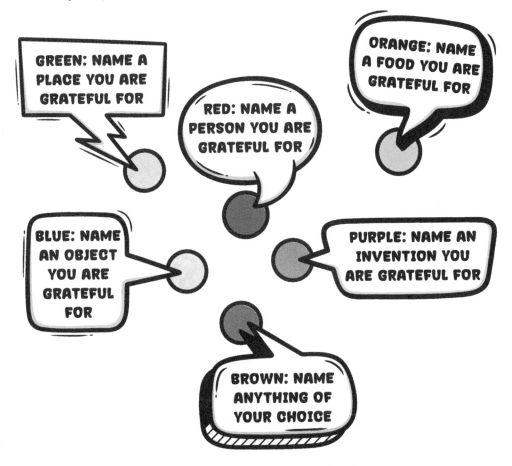

Gratitude Dice Game

Gratitude means taking time to notice and appreciate the big and small things in life.

This easy and fun dice game is great for connecting with friends and family through gratitude.

Cut and glue to assemble your 10-sided dice. Roll the dice and take turns answering the questions.

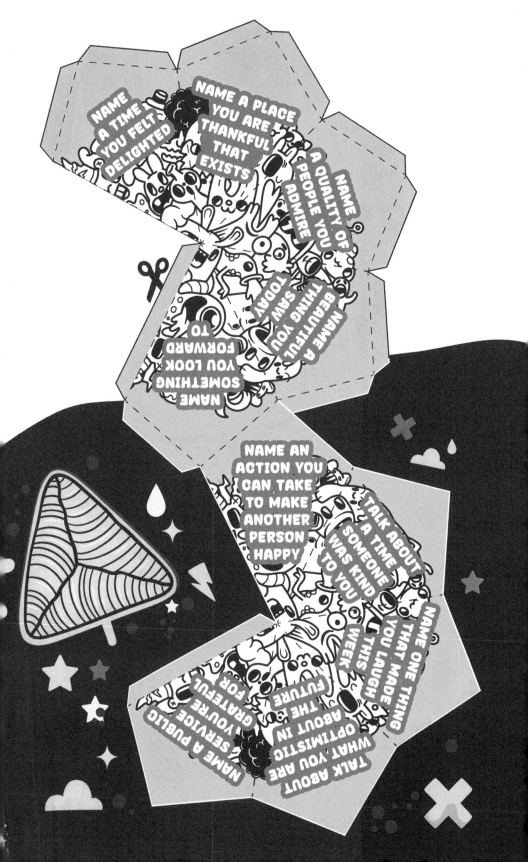

Your journey in completing *The Gratitude Game: A Journal for Young Teens and Adults.*

As the creator of the Gratitude Game, I have firsthand experience with the transformative power of gratitude. I remember a specific time when gratitude helped me navigate a difficult situation. I was excited to join my boyfriend for a holiday after a long separation. I packed my bags and headed to the long-haul bus station. As I was getting on the bus with my backpack and a small purse, the bus driver told me only one bag was allowed and physically pushed me off the bus, closed the door and drove away. I was devastated and burst into tears.

After waiting for two hours, I caught a train to meet my boyfriend. Still in tears, I looked out the window and saw a beautiful sunset over a golden field – it was truly stunning.

I was grateful for the opportunity to witness such a beautiful scene. Being grateful helped shift my perspective towards a more positive outlook. To me, gratitude means taking time to appreciate the positive aspects of life. By focusing on things I was grateful for and incorporating gratitude into my daily routine, I was able to cope better with stress and challenging situations, and my overall well-being and satisfaction with life improved.

Feedback is a gift. In my endeavour to create the best quality book, I would love to hear your thoughts and opinions. To do so, I want to ask you for a favour – please leave an honest review of The Gratitude Game on Amazon. Tell me and other potential journal-keepers what you liked, what you wished for, and what you wondered about. Your review will give me the feedback I need to improve. Feedback is essential for learning and growth; we cannot improve without it.

I hope your experience with The Gratitude Game was positive and memorable. Thank you in advance for your valuable feedback.

In gratitude,

Sandy Lam

Achor, S. (2013). Before happiness the 5 Hidden Keys to Achieving success, Spreading happiness, and Sustaining Positive change. Currency.

Allen, S., Ph.D. (2018). The Science of Gratitude. John Templeton Foundation.

Brown, B. (2021). Atlas of the heart. London: Vermilion.

Burton, L. R. (n.d.). The Neuroscience of Gratitude What you need to know about the new neural knowledge. Wharton Health Care Management Alumni Association. www.whartonhealthcare.org/the_neuroscience_of_gratitude

Eagleman, D., Dr. (2020). Livewired: The Inside Story of the Ever-Changing Brain. Pantheon.

Emmons, R. A., & McCullough, M. E. (2003). Counting blessings versus burdens: An experimental investigation of gratitude and subjective well-being in daily life. Journal of Personality and Social Psychology, 84, 377-389.

Ohio State University. (2020). Gratitude interventions don't help with depression, anxiety: Being grateful has benefits, but not for these issues. ScienceDaily. www.sciencedaily.com/releases/2020/03/200309130010.htm

Emmons, R. A. (2004). The Psychology of Gratitude. Oxford University Press; Annotated Edition.

Emmons, R. A. (2007). Thanks!: How the New Science of Gratitude Can Make You Happier. Houghton Mifflin Harcourt.

Sutton, J., Ph.D. (2019). Letters of Gratitude: How to Write a Message of Appreciation. PositivePsychology.com B.V. www.positivepsychology.com/gratitude-messages-letters-lists/

Stillman, J. (2016). Gratitude Physically Changes Your Brain, New Study Says. Inc. com. www.inc.com/jessica-stillman/the-amazing-way-gratitude-rewires-your-brain-for-happiness.html

Tomasulo, D. (2020). Learned hopefulness: The power of positivity to overcome depression. Oakland: New Harbinger.

Webb, N. (2011). The Neurobiology of Bliss--Sacred and Profane. Scientific American. www.scientificamerican.com/article/the-neurobiology-of-bliss-sacred-and-profane/

Wert, K. (2018). 48 Unconventional things I'm Grateful for ... That I Bet are not on your List! John Templeton Foundation. www.meanttobehappy.com/49-unconventional-things-im-grateful-for-that-i-bet-are-not-on-your-list/

Vincent, G. (2018). The Neurobiology of Bliss. Medium. www.medium.com/betahuman/the-neurobiology-of-bliss-ed23e89a1f9f

(n.d.). Gratitude and Depression: Can Gratefulness Make You Happy? Pasadena Villa Psychiatric Treatment Network. www.pasadenavilla.com/resources/blog/gratitude-and-depression/

Made in the USA
Las Vegas, NV
05 October 2024

96323223R10066